BUDO
secrets

Fudo Myo-o, the patron saint of Budo. *Fudo* means "immovable," "unshakable," "imperturbable," symbolizing the steadfastness and resolve needed by martial artists. *Myo-o* is "king of light," indicating the enlightenment that is manifested on the highest level of mastery. Fudo wields the sword of instructive wisdom and holds a lasso to bind evildoers who fail to heed the message. (Painting, with the Fudo Sutra as an inscription, by Tesshu Yamaoka.)

佛說聖不動經

爾時大會中有一明王是大明王有大
威力大悲徳故現青黒形大定徳故坐金
盤石大智恵故現大火焔執大智剣害貪瞋
癡持三昧索縛難伏者無相法身虚空同体
無其住処但住衆生心想之中衆生意想各各不同
隨衆生意而作利益所求圓満爾時大會聞説是經
皆大歓喜信受奉行

昭和二十一年三月

山田氏

TEACHINGS OF THE
MARTIAL ARTS MASTERS

EDITED BY John Stevens

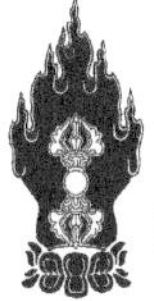

Shambhala · Boston & London · 2002

Shambhala Publications, Inc.
Horticultural Hall
300 Massachusetts Avenue
Boston, Massachusetts 02115
www.shambhala.com

15 14 13 12 11 10 9 8

Printed in the United States of America
♾ This edition is printed on acid-free paper that meets the American National Standards Institute z39.48 Standard.
♻ Shambhala Publications makes every effort to print on recycled paper. For more information please visit www.shambhala.com.
Distributed in the United States by Penguin Random House LLC and in Canada by Random House of Canada Ltd

ART CREDITS

Art on pages 33 and 43 appears courtesy of Samuel Bercholz.
Art on pages 84–85 appears courtesy of Eisei Bunko.
Art on page 93 appears courtesy of Belinda Sweet.
Art on page 95 appears courtesy of Hiroshi Komatsu.
Art on page 96 appears courtesy of Tusha Buntin.

Interior design and composition: Greta D. Sibley & Associates

The Library of Congress catalogues the hardcover edition of this book as follows:

Budo secrets: teachings of the martial arts masters/edited by John Stevens.—1st ed.
p. cm.
Includes index.
ISBN 978-1-57062-446-9 (hardcover)
ISBN 978-1-57062-915-0 (pbk.)
1. Martial arts—Japan—Philosophy. I. Stevens, John, 1947–

GV1100.77.A2 B84 2001
796.8′0952—dc21
00-054771

CONTENTS

PART TWO

the philosophy of budo

PART THREE

tales of the masters of budo

PREFACE

The Japanese word *budo* consists of two characters. Although usually translated as "martial," the original components of the character *bu* have the meaning "to stop clashing weapons," with a definite connotation of restoring peace. *Bu* may also be interpreted as "valorous action," "courageous living," and "commitment to justice." *Do* is Tao, "the Way to truth," "the Path to liberation." The two concepts merge as budo, "the Way of brave and enlightened activity."

Budo Secrets: Teachings of the Martial Arts Masters consists of three sections. The first is a collection of the principles of budo, taken from various training manuals and transmission scrolls. The second section contains excerpts on the philosophical elements of budo, including the seminal text *Neko no Myojutsu,* "The Marvelous Techniques of the Old Cat." The third section relates instructional tales told of the budo masters. Since many of the budo masters were excellent calligraphers and painters and used brush and ink as a teaching medium, I have also included a number of illustrations by different martial artists.

In keeping with tradition, I have kept additional commentary to a minimum. Budo texts and tales are meant to be cryptic. They are not for "dummies" or "idiots." They are to be understood through lifelong personal experience and self-reflection, through discussion with fellow trainees, and through person-to-person, heart-to-heart transmission from a teacher.

As I note several times in the text, the teachings of budo are still actively studied today, and they are not to be dismissed as relics of a different age. In fact, Morihei Ueshiba, the founder of Aikido, told his disciples that true budo was finally emerging in the present era. May it be so!

John Stevens
Sendai, 2001

TRANSLATOR'S NOTE

Names of premodern Japanese figures are given in the traditional Japanese manner; the names of postmodern (1868 and later) figures are given Western style, with family name second. Dates are supplied when known.

the principles *of budo*

Three essential elements of budo are: the timing of heaven, the utility of earth, and the harmonization of human beings.

—BUGEI KODEN

Izanami (*left,* holding a moon spear) and Izanagi (*right,* holding a sun spear), the Shinto couple of creation, from a secret transmission scroll of the Shinkage School. Integration—between male and female elements, yin and yang, self and other—is one key to budo secrets.

イサナキ
平法
口傳種々
イサナミ

Ki-ichi-Hogen's Secrets of Technique

The "Secrets of Technique" were said to have been passed to Ushiwakamaru (known also as Minamoto Yoshitsune, 1159–1189) by the mysterious master Ki-ichi-Hogen. These teachings have been widely employed by martial art instructors over the centuries and are still in use. Morihei Ueshiba (1888–1969), the founder of Aikido, often quoted from this list when teaching and demonstrating Aikido techniques, and so did my Aikido teacher Rinjiro Shirata (1912–1993).

When your opponent comes, greet him at once.

If he withdraws, immediately send him on his way.

When there is opposition, harmonize with it on the spot.

If there is a force of one, add nine to make ten.

If there is a force of two, add eight to make ten.

If there is a force of five, add five to make ten.

Utilize this principle to achieve harmonization.

There is nothing in the universe that cannot be harmonized.

Distinguish between truth and falsehood.

Know how to discern the hidden.

Great is larger than the universe.

Small enters the tiniest particle.

Adjust to the vagaries of life and death.

Adapt to ceaseless change.

Remain unshaken regardless of the circumstances.

Miyamoto Musashi's Self-Precepts and Nine Articles

The celebrated swordsman and Zen artist Miyamoto Musashi (1584–1645) formulated a series of self-precepts that he grouped under the title *Following the Solitary Path*. The precepts are austere and uncompromising, as is to be expected of a wandering samurai who devoted himself to the forging of mind and body. There are two versions of *Following the Solitary Path*: one containing nineteen precepts and one containing twenty-one. The older, and longer, version is given here.

Do not violate the laws of society.

Do not seek comfort for your person.

Do not play favorites (be free of bias).

Think lightly of yourself and deeply about worldly affairs.

Do not have many desires throughout your life.

Have no regrets regarding personal affairs.

Do not be jealous or envious of others' affairs.

Do not grieve when you have to separate yourself from something or someone.

Do not begrudge yourself or others.

Do not think about falling in love.

Do not become infatuated with physical objects.

Do not wish to settle down.

Do not take fine food for yourself.

Do not pile up possessions.

Do not overvalue the things you have.

Do not become obsessed with having splendid weapons.

When following the Way, do not be afraid of dying.

Do not hoard money for your old age.

Venerate buddhas and gods but do not rely on them.

Abandon self-interest, and do not seek fame or fortune.

Never separate yourself from the Way of a Warrior.

In the "Earth" chapter of the *Book of Five Rings,* Musashi lists Nine Articles for those who wish to follow his strategy.

1. Do not think dishonestly.
2. Constantly forge body and mind.
3. Become acquainted with all the arts.
4. Know something about every craft.
5. Learn to gauge the merits and demerits of things.
6. Develop understanding of all matters.
7. Perceive things that are not obvious.
8. Pay attention to the smallest details.
9. Do not waste time on nonessentials.

Seven Hardships for Martial Training

While Miyamoto Musashi's precepts are admittedly austere, they are not as extreme as those listed in a text called *Bukyo Shigen Goden Ryu.*

SEVEN HARDSHIPS FOR MARTIAL TRAINING

1. Experience cold, heat, and rain by scaling high mountains and crossing deep valleys.
2. Rest in open fields, and sleep in the mountains.
3. Never store money or food, and never wear warm clothes.
4. Travel everywhere to engage in contests.
5. Reside in graveyards, haunted houses, or among wild beasts.
6. Associate with dangerous criminals.
7. Live off the land among peasants.

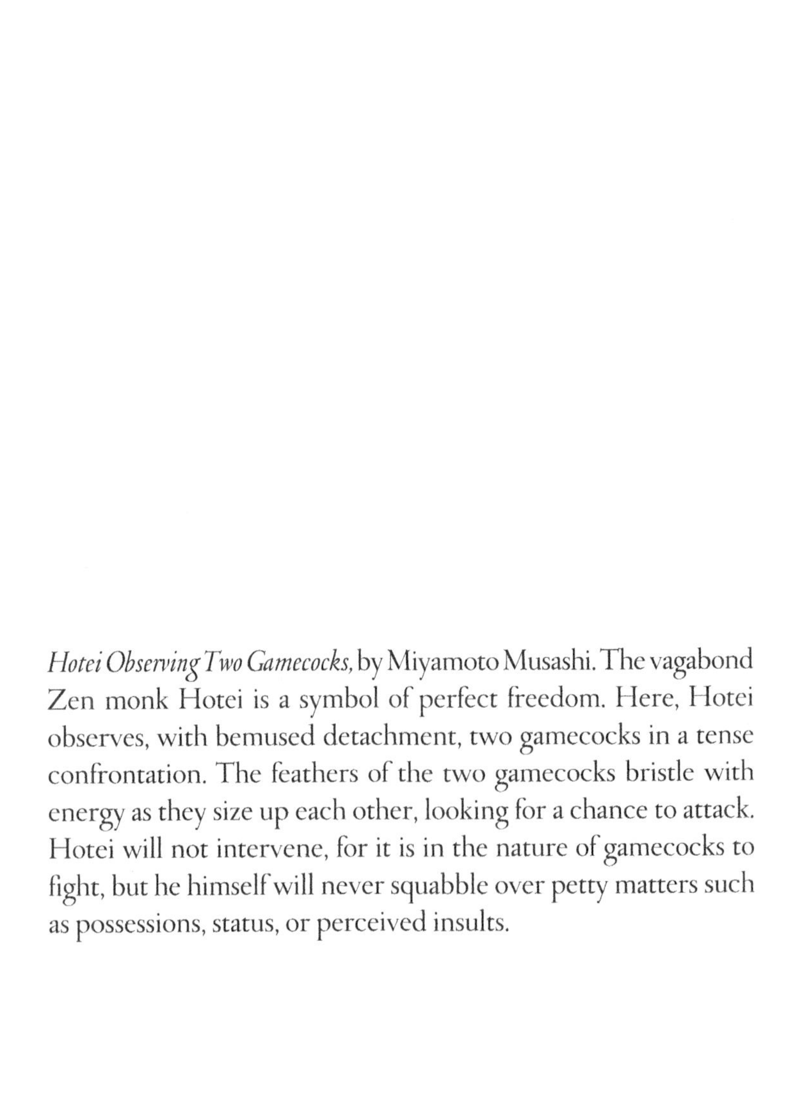

Hotei Observing Two Gamecocks, by Miyamoto Musashi. The vagabond Zen monk Hotei is a symbol of perfect freedom. Here, Hotei observes, with bemused detachment, two gamecocks in a tense confrontation. The feathers of the two gamecocks bristle with energy as they size up each other, looking for a chance to attack. Hotei will not intervene, for it is in the nature of gamecocks to fight, but he himself will never squabble over petty matters such as possessions, status, or perceived insults.

Furious Frog, by Hirayama Shiryu (1759–1828). Long ago, a Chinese emperor was leading his troops to an important battle when he noticed a tiny frog puffed up and ready to attack the huge intruders on his territory. Impressed by the frog's fighting spirit, the emperor admonished his men to display similar determination in facing their foes.

Shiryu was a genuine old-time martial artist. He kept away from women, slept in the training hall, wore one thin robe all year long, and rose at 4:00 A.M. to practice martial arts—Shiryu was said to have mastered eighteen different kinds. Following morning training, Shiryu studied military manuals. As he read, Shiryu would crush unhulled chestnuts and punch and stab at a wooden board to toughen his hands and fingers. When Shiryu brushed calligraphy such as this, he would let out a terrific shout and then attack the paper.

Yagyu Renya's Seven Principles

Yagyu Renya (1625–1694) was one of the illustrious swordsmen produced by the famous Yagyu clan. He started training at an early age under the tutelage of his father, Toshiyoshi, and other Yagyu relatives. Renya retired from active training and teaching at age sixty and took vows as a Buddhist monk. Like Musashi, Renya never married, and in fact stated that a man who wanted to master swordsmanship should stay as far away as possible from women. Renya loved to garden and it is said that he designed several gardens in the Owari district. The accompanying explanations of Renya's principles are based on traditional commentaries.

1. STAY IN THE CENTER

   This is the principle of the golden mean: stay in the physical center of a place, and stay centered in body and mind.

2. EMPTY SWORD (LEARN TO MAKE THE FAR COME NEAR)

   This is the same state as that of "no-sword." If the

mind is empty, and not fixed on a particular set of circumstances such as near or far, one can act spontaneously and bring every attack into one's own sphere.

3. CUT OFF SELF (DO NOT ATTACK YOUR OPPONENT)

As soon as the desire to win emerges, one loses perspective and attempts to force the issue, which can result in defeat.

4. HARMONIZE THE *HARA* AND THE *SENAKA* (FRONT AND BACK ARE A SINGLE SURFACE)

This means to employ the entire body as a unified whole in a rhythmic manner.

5. FORGET YOUR BODY

It is not good to be overly conscious of one's physical condition, especially aches and pains, nor to rigidly adhere to a particular stance and attitude.

6. GREET YOUR OPPONENT

When an attack does arise, move to meet it swiftly, boldly, and fearlessly. Or better still, make your opponent feel welcome to attack, then capture his spirit when he enters your sphere.

7. PRACTICE BY YOURSELF

This means both to practice by oneself (early in the morning and late at night) and to practice the preceding six principles at all times—standing or sitting, awake or asleep, in public and in private.

Three Rules of the Tanseki School of Swordsmanship

Much about the Tanseki School of Swordsmanship is obscure, but its manual, *Tanseki Ryu Densho*, is still studied. The following set of "The Three Rules for Practice" are taken from that manual. The first joy, "vicissitude," means that ceaseless change brings many challenges to face, thus widening one's experience and increasing the quality of one's training.

THE THREE PROHIBITIONS

1. To give up
2. To misbehave
3. To be clumsy

THE THREE JOYS

1. Vicissitude
2. Honesty
3. Skillfulness

THE THREE EVILS

1. Fear
2. Doubt
3. Confusion

The Eight Essentials for Novice Swordsmen

New trainees were told to memorize these eight essential points regarding swordsmanship and then apply them in practice both in and out of the training hall.

1. Treat every encounter as a fight to the finish.
2. Carefully observe your opponent's deportment.
3. Gauge the level of your opponent's ability.
4. Allow for unexpected behavior by your opponent.
5. Adjust the distance (physical and mental) between you and your opponent accordingly.
6. Draw your opponent out and bring him into your own sphere.
7. When you cannot defeat your opponent physically, attempt to trick him psychologically.
8. When your opponent is of exceptional ability, do not challenge him directly. Devise a different strategy.

Demons stay away!
Shoki is on guard in emptiness!

Kamae in Japanese means both "stance" and "attitude." Here, Shoki the Demon-queller, a popular folk god, displays an intensely dynamic stance, ready to overpower an opponent. (Painting by Tesshu.)

Don't hold back
Trying to protect your ass;
As soon as an
opening appears,
seize it!

Unlike Shoki the Demon-queller, this *kappa* (mythical water sprite) assumes a totally relaxed natural stance. Once an opening in an opponent's defense appears, however, the kappa will leap into action. (Kappas like to snatch their opponent's liver through the anus.) In budo, one needs to be able to assume either stance, depending on the circumstances. (Painting by Tesshu.)

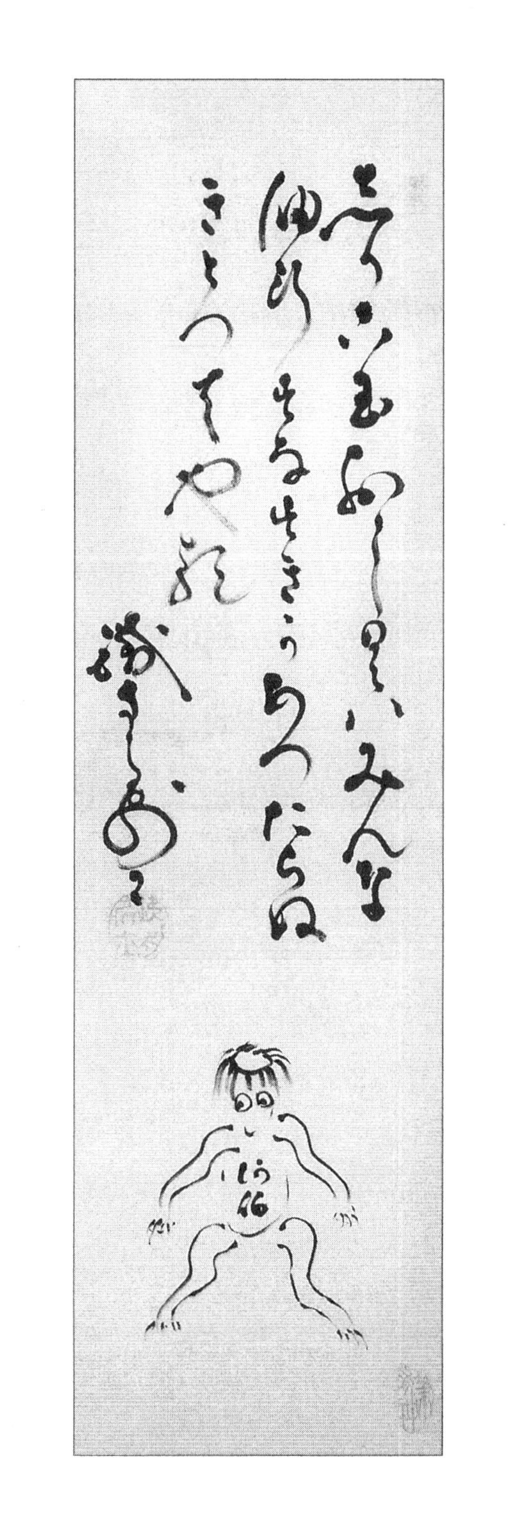

Gichin Funakoshi's Twenty Principles of Karate

Gichin Funakoshi (1868-1957), the father of modern Karate, was born in Okinawa. He was one of the first Okinawan masters to teach Karate on the Japanese mainland, where he established the Shotokan School in Tokyo. Funakoshi summed up his views on the Way of Karate in twenty principles.

1. Never forget that Karate begins and ends with respect.
2. There is no first attack in Karate.
3. Karate fosters righteousness.
4. First know yourself, and then know others.
5. Rather than physical technique, mental technique.
6. Let your mind roam freely.
7. Inattention and neglect cause misfortune.
8. Never think that Karate is practiced only in the training hall.

9. Karate is a lifelong pursuit.
10. Everything you encounter is an aspect of Karate; find the marvelous truth there.
11. Karate is like boiling water; if you do not keep the flame high (with continual training), it turns tepid.
12. Do not think about winning; think about not losing.
13. Respond in accordance to your opponent.
14. Wage the battle with natural strategy.
15. Regard your hands and feet as weapons.
16. Step out the door and you face 10,000 foes.
17. Learn various stances as a beginner, but then rely on a natural posture.
18. The traditional forms must be practiced correctly; real combat is another matter.
19. Never forget your own strengths and weaknesses, the limitations of your body, and the relative quality of your techniques.
20. Continually polish your mind.

Tando, "Search for the Way," by Jigoro Kano (1860–1938), founder of Kodokan Judo. Kano established his system of budo by thoroughly researching the martial traditions of both East and West. Kano formulated "Five Principles of Judo":

1. Carefully observe oneself and one's situation, carefully observe others, and carefully observe one's environment.
2. Seize the initiative in whatever you undertake.
3. Consider fully, act decisively.
4. Know when to stop.
5. Keep to the middle.

Kyuzo Mifune's Principles of Judo

Kyuzo Mifune (1883-1965) was perhaps the greatest Judo master of the modern era. Only about five feet four inches tall and less than 140 pounds in weight, Mifune could easily defeat opponents twice his size. There is a wonderful film of Mifune at age seventy-three facing off against a series of big and powerful young foreign and Japanese Judo artists, and he tosses each of them about in turn. Mifune said that the key to training was simply hard work: "If my opponents train one hour, I will train two. If they train two hours, I will train three." Mifune trained even when injured: "I learned to use the parts of my body that were not injured." His favorite technique was *kuki-nage*, or "air-throw," based on the principle of the sphere: a sphere never loses its center, it moves swiftly without strain, and it does not resist force.

THE FIVE PRINCIPAL POINTS OF JUDO

1. The soft controls the hard.
2. Strike to kill (resolve any problem with a single decisive action).

3. Do not hold anything back (never be tentative).
4. Enter a state of no-self, no-mind.
5. Do not place hope in finding a secret technique. Polish the mind through ceaseless training; that is the key to effective techniques.

SEVEN RULES OF JUDO PRACTICE

1. Do not make light of an opponent.
2. Do not lose self-confidence.
3. Maintain a good posture.
4. Develop speed.
5. Project power in all directions.
6. Never stop training.
7. Develop self-control.

THE SONG OF JUDO

When you train, free yourself from distracting thoughts;
Keep your heart buoyant, your body buoyant, too.
Do not forget the principle of "return to the center";
Strive and strive, with single-minded devotion.
This is the true path of softness!
This is the true path of softness!

Accumulate skill through ceaseless forging of body
and mind;
Attain the miraculous power of seven times down, eight
times up.

Become enlightened to the path of liberation;
Become like a rotating ball, effortlessly responding to any
contingency.
This is the true path of softness!
This is the true path of softness!

The path of softness transcends national borders:
A pliant heart has no enemies.
People of the world join hands,
And establish an ideal global village.
This is the true path of softness!
This is the true path of softness!

Shojin, "Constant Effort," by Kyuzo Mifune. Along with constant training, Mifune emphasized the virtue of gratitude. He once said, "I'm grateful to my parents for giving me a small body. In order to overcome bigger opponents, I had to train twice as hard."

Seven Times Down, Eight Times Up!—Daruma doll by Deiryu (1895-1954). Daruma dolls that spring right back up are popular in Japan, and the dolls impart an important message: No matter how often you are knocked down by failure, get up and try again. This is essential in budo, where one often finds oneself on the ground. Deiryu was one of the more outstanding Zen monks of the twentieth century—a master of calligraphy, the tea ceremony, and *kyudo* (archery).

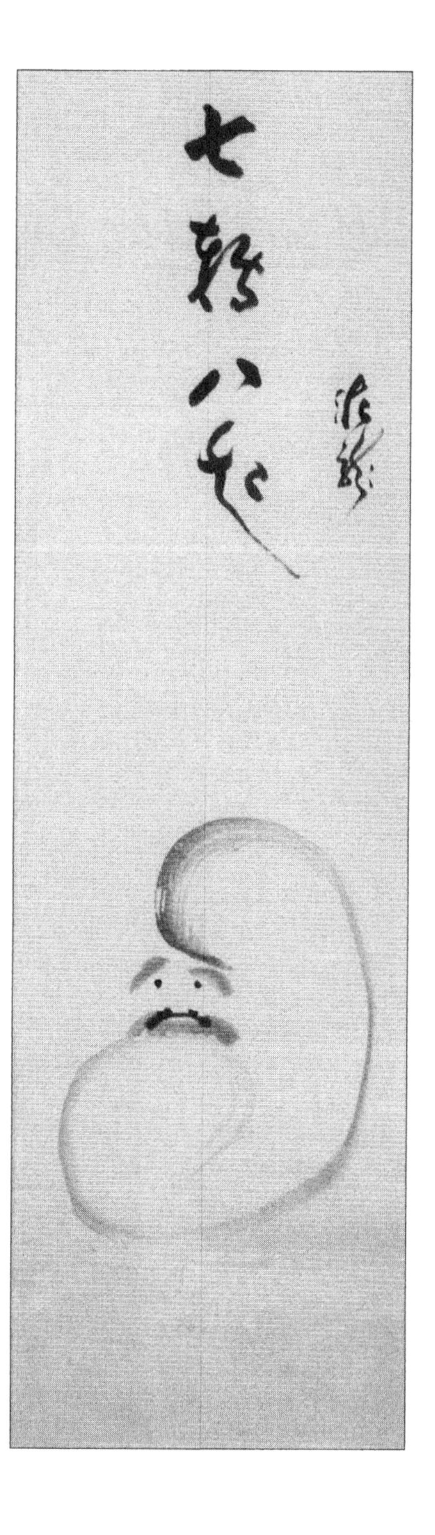

Twenty Rules for Lifelong Training

Early in their formal education, young samurai were instructed by their mentors to brush a copy of these rules and then sign and date the document as a lifelong pledge.

1. Never lie.
2. Never forget to be grateful to one's Lord.
3. Never forget to be grateful to one's parents.
4. Never forget to be grateful to one's teachers.
5. Never forget to be grateful to one's fellow human beings.
6. Do nothing to offend gods, buddhas, and one's elders.
7. Do not begrudge small children.
8. Do not burden others with your own troubles.
9. There is no place for anger and rage in the Way.
10. Do not rejoice at the misfortune of others.

11. Do your best to do what is best.
12. Do not turn your back on others and only think of yourself.
13. When you eat, be mindful of the hard work of the farmers who grew the food. Never be wasteful of plants, trees, earth, or stones.
14. Do not dress up in fine clothes, or waste time on superficial appearance.
15. Always behave properly with good manners.
16. Always treat everyone like an honored guest.
17. To overcome ignorance, learn from as many people as possible.
18. Do not study and practice the arts just to make a name for yourself.
19. Human beings have good and bad points. Do not dismiss or laugh at anyone.
20. Strive to behave well but keep good actions hidden and do not seek the praise of others.

The Ten Virtues for a Ninja

Ninja are often viewed as medieval Japanese assassins—masters of stealth, deception, and mayhem—but several schools of ninjutsu aspired to maintain samurai ethical standards. The following list is from the ninja text *Bankawa Shukai.*

1. Loyalty
2. Bravery
3. Strategic Knowledge
4. Diligence
5. Trustworthiness
6. Good health
7. Responsibility
8. Ingenuity
9. Knowledge of the Teachings of Buddha and Confucius
10. Gifted Speech

Ninja Food for Training

Ninja were legendary for their strength, agility, and stamina. What kind of food fueled their training? Ninja food had eight requirements.

It must be light in weight.

It must not be bulky.

It must not spoil easily.

It must be rather tasty.

It must be locally grown and readily available.

It must be inexpensive.

It must be simple to prepare.

It must make one feel full even in a small amount.

The Ten Evils for a Budo Practitioner

This list comes from a Kashima Shin School scroll. Martial artist or not, all of us would do well to overcome each of these evils—evils that reflect defects in one's character.

1. Insolence
2. Overconfidence
3. Greed
4. Anger
5. Fear
6. Doubt
7. Distrust
8. Hesitation
9. Contempt
10. Conceit

The Book of the Heart

This short document, called *Kokoro no maki* in Japanese, was often included in budo manuals. *Kokoro* means "heart," "center," "core."

When the heart is full of things, the body feels constrained; when it is empty, the body feels expansive.

When there is too much reserve in the heart, love and respect are lost; when it is free of reserve, love and respect are gained.

When the heart is full of base passion, principles are forgotten; when it is free of base passion, principles are remembered.

When the heart is set on gaudy things, appearances are falsified; when it is free of artifice, appearances are real.

When the heart is full of pride, others are begrudged; when it is free of pride, others are respected.

When the heart is full of oneself, others are doubted; when it is selfless, others are trusted.

When the heart is full of error, others appear frightening; when it is free of error, there is nothing to fear.

When the heart is full of obstructions, others are harmed; when it is free of obstructions, no one is harmed.

When the heart is full of covetousness, others are flattered; when it is free of covetousness, there is no need to flatter.

When the heart is full of anger, words are spoken harshly; when it is free of anger, words are pacific.

When the heart is full of patience, everything can be set in order; when it is not patient, everything collapses.

When the heart is full of self-importance, the goodness of others is ignored; when it is free of self-importance, the goodness of others is appreciated.

When the heart is full of greed, requests are endless; when it is free of greed, nothing extra is required.

When the heart is full of illusion, others are blamed; when it is free of illusion, no one is scorned.

When the heart is full of sincerity, contentment is easy; when it is not sincere, there will be no contentment.

Kokoro, by D. T. Suzuki (1871–1966). Suzuki included two long chapters on Zen and the art of swordsmanship in his finest and most influential book, *Zen and Japanese Culture.*

The Nine Views

Based on the teachings of Zen Buddhism, this is a traditional form of meditation taught to samurai. The accompanying comments are my own, based on traditional written and oral instruction.

1. OBSERVE THE FUNDAMENTAL RULES

   There is an etiquette to sitting meditation. One can sit either in *seiza* (formal Japanese style on the knees), in the lotus posture, or in a straight-backed chair. One first needs to learn the rules for a proper meditation posture.

2. BREATHE FROM THE BELLY

   The breath should be centered in the *kikai tanden,* a point about two inches beneath the navel. Breathing should be slow, rhythmic, and calm.

3. SOOTHE THE SPIRIT

   As one settles down, petty thoughts, distracting

emotions, and mental agitation should gradually melt away.

4. FULFILLMENT

As worldly thoughts dissipate, one should fill the body with *ki* (life force) from the top of one's head to the bottom of one's feet. There should be a sense of completeness.

5. NATURAL WISDOM

If one is calm, undisturbed, and unagitated, things can be seen in their true light, and this leads to the development of natural wisdom.

6. LIBERATION

This means not to get caught up or snared by any particular object, physical or mental. It is a state of freedom.

7. TRUE VOID

Just like a cloudless sky, the mind is clear and bright—its true state. Usually the limitless sky is obscured by clouds, sometimes very dark and thick, and this makes human beings downcast. Penetrate the clouds, however, and the light can be seen in full glory.

8. MARVELOUS FUNCTION

For a realization to be authentic, one must be able to apply it in the actual world. True understanding is reflected in one's technique and also in one's daily life. This is the real battlefield where one's enlightenment is constantly tested.

9. PERFECTION

   The Japanese term for this final "view" is *enso,* the "circle of Zen." The circle is both perfectly empty and perfectly full; it is simultaneously transcendent and immanent.

Proper understanding of these "Nine Views" leads to the insight that "the way of heaven is to achieve victory without fighting."

Enso, "Zen Circle of Enlightenment," by Motsugai (see page 89). Many budo manuals represent the ultimate teaching as a circle (or sphere). It is empty yet full, perfect, complete, radiant. Although Motsugai was famed as a strongman—he could lift huge temple bells and dent a hardwood *go* board with his fist—his brushwork is soft, supple, and settled.

the philosophy *of budo*

All things have an inner divine essence and an outer marvelous function. The essence of a tree is manifested in its wonderful blossoms and abundant foliage. The essence of tree could not be perceived if there were no blossom and leaves. Human beings have an inner divine essence that cannot be seen but is manifested as the marvelous techniques of budo.

—HEIHO JIKANSHO OF THE KAJIMA SHINTO SCHOOL

The Marvelous Techniques of the Old Cat

(Neko no Myojutsu)

Neko no Myojutsu, "The Marvelous Techniques of the Old Cat," first appeared in a collection of essays titled *Inaka Soshi* ("The Country Taoist"), written in 1727 by the scholar Issai Chozan (Tanba Jurozaemon Tadaaki, 1659–1741). It became a very popular text among martial artists and remains so—it was one of the writings we studied during the intensive training sessions conducted by the Jikishin-kage School of Swordsmanship that I attended.

There once was a swordsman named Shoken. His home was plagued by a huge rat who roamed around freely, even during the day. Shoken's house cat was no match for the rat and fled in terror after being severely bitten. Shoken acquired several tough local polecats to combat the rat in a group. They were released in the house, and went for the rat, who crouched in a corner of a room waiting for them to come. The rat lashed out ferociously at one cat after the other and drove them all off.

Angered by the abject failure of all the cats, the master

decided to dispatch the rat with his sword. Despite his skill as a swordsman, he could not strike the rat—the animal leaped great distances through the air, moved like lightning, and boldly leaped right over the top of the swordsman's head. Shoken gave up in exasperation and decided to seek the aid of the Amazing Old Cat from a nearby village.

When the owner brought the Old Cat over to Shoken's house, Shoken was surprised at how ordinary and aged the cat appeared. However, he said, "Let's give it a try," and released the cat into the room where the rat was ensconced. As soon as it saw the cat approach, the rat froze. The cat nonchalantly walked over, seized the rat by the neck, carried it out of the room, and turned it over to Shoken.

That night, the other cats gathered and gave the Old Cat the seat of honor. They said to him, "We are well known for our skill in rat catching, able to handle even weasels and otters, and our nails are razor sharp. However, there was nothing we could do against that rat. How was it that you were able to overcome that giant rat? Please impart to us the secrets of your art."

The Old Cat laughed and said, "Well, you are all still young and although you have had experience in fighting with rats you still have a lot to learn. Before I begin, though, tell me about your training."

A black cat came forward and said, "I was raised in a family that specialized in training cats. I was taught how to leap over a seven-foot screen, how to squeeze into tiny holes, and all kinds of acrobatic tricks. I was an expert at feigning sleep and then striking out as soon as a rat came near. Rats could not escape me. I could catch them even as they fled across ceiling beams. I was never defeated until I met that old rat."

The Old Cat said, "Your training has centered exclusively on technique. All you think about is catching the rat. The old masters taught patterns and movements to enable us to develop good technique. And even the simplest technique contains profound principles. You focus on external technique too much. That causes you to doubt the traditions of the masters and to devise new tricks. However, if you rely on technique too much, sooner or later you will come to an impasse because physical technique has a limit. Ponder this well."

Next the tiger cat stepped forward and said: "I think that the development of *ki* (life force) is most important. I have polished my ki for many years, and my spirit is very strong, filling heaven and earth. I could face down my opponents with overwhelming ki and defeat them from the start. I could immediately respond to any stimulus, any movement. I did not need to think; techniques naturally arose. I could freeze a rat running across a beam and make it drop to the floor. That old rat, though, came without a form, and left not a trace. I was stymied."

The old cat replied, "The ki power you use is still a function of your own mind, and thus too self-centered. It is based entirely on your own level of self-confidence. As long as you remain conscious of your ki power and use it mentally to suppress an opponent, you will create resistance. And you will be sure to meet an opponent whose ki power is even stronger than yours. You may think that your ki power fills the universe in the same manner as the *kozen no ki* (universal energy) employed by the Chinese sage Mencius, but it does not. In the case of Mencius, ki is bright and vigorous. His use of ki power is like a great river; your use of ki power is like a flash flood. We all know the proverb 'A biting cat gets bitten by the rat.' When a rat is cornered it forgets life, forgets desires, forgets winning and losing, forgets body and mind. That force is as strong as steel, and it cannot be vanquished merely by ki power."

Next, an older gray cat advanced quietly and said, "As you have stated, that type of ki power can be very strong but it still retains a form, however slight, that can be used against you. As for me, for many years now I have been polishing my heart. I do not rely solely on ki power, I never harbor thoughts of fighting with an opponent, and always try to harmonize myself to any attack. When an opponent is strong, I blend and follow his movements. My technique is like that of a curtain capturing and dropping to the floor a stone thrown against it. Until now, even the strongest rat could find no place to attack me. This rat, though, was amazing—ki power and harmonizing power had no effect on it."

The Old Cat answered, "Your harmonizing power is not the harmonizing power of nature. It is a projection of your own mind and thus limited. Any trace of conscious thought destroys your equilibrium, and a sharp opponent will seize on that opening in an instant. Thought obstructs nature and hinders true function. Do not think, do not act; follow the movements of nature, and self will disappear. Without a self, there will be no one to oppose you in Heaven and Earth.

"It is not my intention to dismiss all of your hard training as worthless. 'The Way has many vessels.' Techniques contain universal principles. Ki power makes the body function and vivifies the cosmos. Harmonizing power enables one to blend naturally with any attacking force, even rocks, without being broken.

"As soon as there is the slightest conscious thought, however, contrivance and willfulness appear, and that separates you from the natural Way. You see yourself and others as separate entities, as opponents. If you ask me what technique I employ, the answer is *mushin* (no-mind). *Mushin* is to act in accordance with nature, nothing else. The Way has no limits, so do not think of this talk of mine as the ultimate secret.

"Long ago, there was a cat in my neighborhood who seemed to do nothing but nap all day. The cat looked spiritless, almost like a cat made out of wood. No one ever saw it catch a rat, yet wherever it was and wherever it went, no rat dared to appear. I once visited the cat and asked it to explain the reason. I asked four times for an answer but it remained silent. It was not that the cat did not want to answer but rather that it did not know how to answer. As the old saying goes, 'Those who know, do not speak; those who speak, do not know.' That cat forgot about itself, forgot about objects, and dwelled in a state of purposelessness. That cat actualized the divine martial virtue of 'non-killing.' I am still no match for that cat."

Shoken, who had been eavesdropping on this dreamlike conversation, suddenly could not contain himself and burst into the room. "I have been training in swordsmanship for many years but I have yet to penetrate its essence. Tonight I have heard about many different kinds of training and learned much about my own Way of the Sword. Please teach me your innermost secrets."

The Old Cat replied: "That I cannot do. I am just an animal that catches rats for food. What do I know about human affairs? I have this to say, though. Swordsmanship is not solely a matter of attaining victory over an opponent. At a critical juncture it is the art of illuminating life and death. Samurai need to foster this attitude of mind and discipline themselves in that spirit. Penetrate the principle of life and death, first of all, and maintain that spirit. Then there will be no doubts, no distracting thoughts, no calculation, no deliberation. Your spirit will remain calm and peaceful, unobstructed, freely responding to any contingency. Conversely, if there is the slightest object in your mind, there will be a self, there will be an enemy, there will be opposition, there will be a loss of freedom. You will enter the darkness of death and lose the spiritual brightness. How can you expect to face an opponent in such a state? Even if you win, it is a shallow victory, and not true swordsmanship. Purposelessness is not a vacant state. It is formless, harboring no objects. If something is harbored there, ki power gathers around it. Ki power is thus stifled and movement becomes stagnant, unbalanced, and uncontrolled. What I call 'purposelessness' harbors nothing, relies on nothing, has no enemy, has no self; it responds to everything naturally and leaves not a trace.

"The *I Ching* states, 'Without thought, without doing, naturally settled, the Way activates itself throughout the universe.' Swordsmen who understand this principle are close to the Way."

Shoken asked, "What is meant by 'There is no enemy, there is no self'?" The Old Cat replied, "Because there is a self, there is an enemy. If there is no self, there is no enemy. 'Enemy' is that which is in opposition. The type of opposition that appears external in yin and yang, fire and water. Every object with form has its opposite. When mind has no form, there is nothing to oppose it. When there is no opposition, there is nothing to fight against. This is called 'no enemy, no self.' When self and objects are both forgotten, there is a natural state of nonactivity, of no trouble, of oneness. The enemy's form is gone, and you know nothing. This is not the same as being unaware; it means no calculating thought, and immediate natural response. This mind is unobstructed and free, allowing the world to become your domain. Abstractions such as 'this,' 'that,' 'like,' and 'dislike' disappear. 'Pleasure and pain, gain and loss' are similar creations of your mind. All of heaven and earth is not to be sought outside of one's own mind.

"An ancient worthy once said, 'A single speck of dust in the eye can make the three worlds look very narrow; liberate your mind and life without obstruction!' When a speck of dust enters the eye it can barely be kept open, and it is difficult to see anything. When something that is bright by nature is contaminated by a foreign object, it loses its clarity. The same holds true for the mind.

"Another ancient said, 'Surrounded by myriad foes, your body may be smashed to pieces, but your mind is yours and it can never be vanquished.' Confucius said, 'Even the meanest human being cannot be deprived of his or her will.' When you are deluded, your own mind becomes your enemy.

"I would like to stop talking here. It is now up to you yourselves. A master can transmit techniques and illuminate the principles behind then, but no more. The truth has to be realized individually. This is self-attainment. It is called 'mind-to-mind transmission,' and 'a separate transmission outside the texts.' While the teaching does not depend on tradition, it utilizes tradition, but still a master cannot impart everything. This is not limited to the study of Zen. From the

Mt. Fuji, by Deishu Takahashi (1835–1903). Deishu, Tesshu's brother-in-law, was a master of the spear and served as a martial arts instructor to the Tokugawa regime. Deishu retired from public life after the Meiji Restoration in 1868, and thereafter devoted himself to poetry composition and calligraphy. He often did paintings of Mt. Fuji, and on one such painting (not this one) Deishu inscribed this poem:

> The towering peak
> Of Mt. Fuji
> Pierces the sky
> But its body remains
> Rooted to earth.

Deishu also wrote: "We do not have a divine body, but compassion can give us a divine body. We do not have divine power, but honesty can give us divine power. We do not have divine intelligence, but wisdom can give us divine intelligence. We cannot perform miracles, but by not creating obstacles we can perform miracles. We cannot save the world, but gentleness will enable us to save the world."

spiritual training methods of the ancient sages to the masterpieces created by artists, all were based on self-attainment and instantaneous mind-to-mind transmission—a teaching outside the texts. The texts teach what you have within and assist you in obtaining it on your own and as your own. A master does not really give you anything. It is easy to talk, and easy to listen, but difficult to perceive these things and make them truly your own. This is called *kensho* (seeing into one's nature) and *satori* (enlightenment). Satori is to awaken from the dream of illusion. It is the same as keen awareness."

In reference to the master cat who seemed to be made of wood, this is a tale from the Taoist classic *Chuang Tzu:*

A king brought a gamecock to a famous trainer. Ten days later, the king asked the trainer how his cock was doing. "The cock is not ready. It is still too aggressive and impetuous." Ten more days passed, and the king inquired again about his cock's progress. "Still not ready," the trainer told him. "The cock tries to intimidate his opponents." Following another ten days, the king came again to check on his cock. "No, not yet," the trainer said. "The cock still gets fighting mad." Finally after yet another ten days, the trainer told the king, "The cock is now ready. It no longer shows any reaction to any of the feints or charges of its opponents. It appears to be a wooden cock until the decisive moment. No other cock will dare to engage him, and they will all run away."

The Secrets of Samurai Swimming

Although budo is typically associated with weapons such as the sword, spear, or bow, swimming was an important martial art. The famous Samurai Training School in Aizu-Wakamatsu had a large pond on the school grounds, and trainees practiced in it every day. The following excerpts are taken from manuals of the Shinden School of Samurai Swimming.

Water is the source of wisdom; swimming is the mother of all the arts.

Children should be introduced to the sea as early as possible. Rather than being strictly "taught" how to float and swim, they should be unobtrusively guided at first in order to allow them to gradually acquaint themselves with the mystery of water.

Body and mind must remain flexible. A calm mind is the single most important element of successful training. A swimmer must avoid struggling against the water, against him- or herself, or against others. A trainee must strive to harmonize him- or herself with the waves, becoming one with the body of water, be it a pond, lake, river, or ocean. Ride the waves with your mind as well as your body.

There are four levels of mastery, symbolized by the four seasons. In spring, the raw swimmer, bursting with energy and eager to compete, needs discipline and hard physical training. In summer, the experienced swimmer, now at his or her physical peak, should explore the full dimensions of the art. In autumn, the mature swimmer can relax a bit, sporting more freely in the water, and reflect on past experiences. By winter, a true swimmer has become a wise old master, beyond the limits of victory or defeat, in perfect harmony with the sea, sky, and shore.

Swimming teaches us how to live properly. There is no way a solitary swimmer can impose his or her selfish will on the water. Swimming against the current will ultimately result in disaster. Swim with the flow without strain, resistance, confusion, or unnatural movement.

Diving fosters bravery; submerging, patience; floating, serenity; distance swimming, fortitude; racing, a fighting spirit; swimming in frigid water, perseverance. A swimmer should practice in all matter of water—seas, lakes, marshes, and rivers—and under all types of conditions—currents, waves, muddy water, and whirlpools.

Here is a related teaching from the *Chuang-tzu*: One day Confucius and his disciples were walking by the Lu Gorge, through which ran a river so turbulent, full of rocks, rapids, and falls that no fish or turtles could sport there. They noticed an old man in the water upstream and then saw him go under. Confucius sent his students downstream to see if they could rescue him from the torrent, but to their surprise the old man suddenly emerged from the water and climbed safely onto the shore. When Confucious asked the old gentleman how he survived in such a raging river, he replied, "I know how to go into a descending vortex and how to come out in an ascending one. I follow the way of the water and do nothing to oppose it. Its nature is my nature."

Tesshu Yamaoka's Secret Art of the Carpenter's Plane

Tesshu Yamaoka (1836–1888)—master of the sword, the brush, and Zen—was the most outstanding martial artist of the nineteenth century. His life and teachings are still avidly studied by modern practitioners of all kinds. This is one of Tesshu's essays on the essence of art.

Use of a carpenter's plane involves three operations: rough, intermediate, and fine. In rough planing the body is braced, the abdomen is tightened, the hips set, equal amounts of strength are put into the hands, and the plane made. In short, strength is put into the entire body and one cannot be slack. If one does not move forcefully, even a rough planing cannot be done.

Next, an intermediate planing is made. This time one must not use all his power. The natural touch of the hands controls increases and decreases in pressure. This level is preparation for the next step. However, if the continuity from rough planing to intermediate planing is broken through a lack of concentration, the work cannot be properly executed.

From intermediate planing one moves to fine planing. Here, irregularities left from the previous steps are smoothed out. If it happens to be a pillar one is working on, one must go from top to bottom with one turn of the plane. While progressing from top to bottom, it is essential to keep the mind in perfect order. If the mind is not in perfect order, various irregularities will appear and the work cannot be completed successfully. Proper control is the key.

Mind, body, and technique must function together in the same manner. "Mind, body, and technique" correspond to "plane, carpenter, and pillar." If one thinks the carpenter does the planing, of what use is the plane? If one thinks the plane does the planing, of what use is the pillar? Mind, body, and technique function together in a way similar to that of plane, carpenter, and pillar; if that interdependence is not understood, one will not be able to produce a good pillar regardless of how long one practices with a carpenter's plane. In order to produce a good pillar, rough planing must be practiced first. Once that step is mastered, the next two steps can be mastered.

Fine planing is the "secret technique." The secret technique is nothing special. Mind, body, and technique are ultimately forgotten and one proceeds smoothly until the work is complete. To no longer think about the results and to no longer talk about the technique or anything else is a marvelous state. It is futile to ask how to attain this—fine planing can be learned only by oneself; it can never be gotten from another.

The Teachings of Tempu Nakamura

Tempu Nakamura (1876-1968) was a popular philosopher who influenced many martial artists, business people, politicians, artists, and writers. After a violent youth—he killed a rival gang leader in self-defense at age sixteen and operated as an espionage agent in Manchuria as a young man—Tempu developed a life-threatening disease at age thirty. Seeking a cure, Tempu traveled the world and eventually cured himself through Yoga. In his mid-forties Tempu became a spiritual teacher, starting out by speaking on street corners. Membership in his association, the Tempu-kai, grew to thousands. Tempu's teaching is simple, direct, and practical.

The most important thing for a human being is not what is between his or her ears; it is what is in his or her heart. If the spirit is strong, one can accomplish anything.

You only live once. Keep yourself in the present. The past is gone, and the future is unknown.

Do not try to cut off all your passions. Passions give birth to heroic activity. Fulfill your passion and that will bring bliss.

Do not think of work—any work—as a duty. If it is a duty, it will become a burden. How do you turn a burden into a pleasure? Live respectfully, correctly, positively, and boldly.

When you rise in the morning, greet the day with vigor. During the day, refrain from thinking or saying, "I'm confused," "I'm weak," "I'm sad," "I need help." At night before you sleep, release all thoughts of sadness, anger, or irritation. Think of pleasant things.

Do not overwork yourself.
Reflect constantly on your state of mind.
Approach others in a positive, bright manner.
Always be grateful, honest, kind, and pleasant.
Speak truly and honestly.

Body and mind form a single entity; life follows basic natural laws that should not be violated.
Your attitude toward life determines its outcome.
The best attitude is based on respect, boldness, truthfulness, and purity.

Foster the life force by being healthy, courageous, decisive, resolute, and vigorous.

Not one thing is an inexhaustible treasure;
There are flowers, there is the moon, and
there is a cherry pavilion.

This calligraphy by Tempu Nakamura is dated "1948, summer" and signed "Philosopher of Unity Tempu." The verse itself is a well-known Zen phrase. One interpretation: "Even though the universe is essentially empty space it produces the most wonderful objects—emptiness is form, form is emptiness."

無一物中無盡藏
有花有月有樓臺

戊子夏
紹一禪人
云風 [illegible]

When you face a stressful situation:
Tighten your anus.
Center yourself in your lower abdomen.
Relax your shoulders.

Teachings of Morihei Ueshiba

After undergoing a profound enlightenment experience at the age of forty-two, Morihei Ueshiba went on to establish Aikido, "The Way of Spiritual Harmony." Morihei's astounding martial feats were without parallel, past or present, but he was also a man of deep religious beliefs, and in his final years Morihei spent much of the training time with his students, expounding his philosophy. The following is a sample of Morihei's wisdom.

The universe is our greatest teacher, our greatest friend. Look at the way a stream wends its way through a mountain valley, smoothly transforming itself as it flows around the rocks. The world's wisdom is contained in books, and by studying them, countless new techniques can be created.

The universe itself is always teaching us Aikido, but we fail to perceive it. Everyone thinks only of him- or herself, and that is why there is so much contention and discord in our world. If we could just keep our hearts pure, everything would be fine. Do not think that the divine exists high above us in heaven. The divine is right here, within and around us. The purpose of Aikido is to remind us that we are in a state of grace.

Aikido is nonviolence. Every human being has been entrusted with a mandate from heaven, and the victory we seek is to overcome all challenges and fight to the finish accomplishing our goals. In Aikido we never attack. If you want to strike first, to gain advantage over someone, that is proof your training is insufficient. Let your partner attack, and use his aggression against him. Do not cower from an attack; control it before it begins.

In true budo, there are no opponents. In true budo we seek to be one with all things, to return to the heart of creation. In real budo, there are no enemies. Real budo is a function of love. The way of a Warrior is not to destroy and kill but to foster life, to continually create. Love is the divinity that can really protect us.

In the old days, a swordsman would let an enemy slice the surface of his skin in order to cut into his enemy's flesh; sometimes he would even sacrifice his flesh in order to slash through to the enemy's bone. In Aikido, such an attitude is unacceptable. We want both attacker and defender to escape unharmed. Rather than risk injury to attain victory, you must learn how to lead your partner. Control an opponent by putting yourself in a secure, safe place.

There is no place in budo for pettiness and selfish thought. Rather than being captivated by notions of "winning or losing," seek the true nature of things. Your thoughts should reflect the grandeur of the universe, a realm beyond life and death. If your thoughts are antagonistic toward the cosmos, those thoughts will destroy you and wreak havoc on the environment.

Masakatsu, "true victory," is associated with the male element of creation; *agatsu,* "self-victory," is associated with the female element. Joined together, they represent *katsuhayabi,* "victory right here, right now!"—an ideal state of perfection and completion.

Masakatsu, "True Victory," by Morihei Ueshiba. Like all great budo masters—Yagyu Munenori once said, "I know not how to defeat others; I only know how to win over myself"—Morihei maintained that the real and most dangerous opponents we face are fear, anger, confusion, doubt, and despair. If we overcome those enemies that attack us from within, we can attain a true victory over any attack from without.

tales of the masters *of budo*

A student asked Jigoro Kano, "What is the secret of Judo?" Kano replied, "Never stop training."

An ardent young man petitioned a master swordsman to accept him as a disciple. "I'll act as your servant and train ceaselessly. How long will it take me to learn everything?"

"At least ten years," the master replied.

"That's too long," the young man protested. "Suppose I work twice as hard as everyone else. Then how long will it take?"

"Thirty years," the master told him.

"What do you mean?" the young man exclaimed. "I'll do anything to master swordsmanship as quickly as possible."

"In that case," the master said sharply, "you will need fifty years. A person in such a hurry is a poor student."

The abashed young man was allowed to serve as an attendant on the condition that he neither ask about nor touch a sword. The young man spent the next three years cleaning, cooking, and running errands. One day, however, the master crept up on the young man and whacked him with a wooden sword. Thereafter, the master continued the sneak attacks day and night until the young man developed an acute sixth sense—he could discern an attack before it was delivered. "Now you are finally ready to learn," the master told him. Formal instruction began and the student made rapid progress.

The master swordsman Tsukahara Bokuden (1490–1572) was on a small ferry boat when a ruffian began boasting of his great prowess with a sword. While the braggart carried on, Bokuden dozed off. This angered the ruffian, who shook Bokuden, demanding to know what style of swordsmanship he followed. Bokuden told him, "The Victory-without-using-the-sword School." The ruffian challenged Bokuden to display such preposterous-sounding swordsmanship. Bokuden agreed, but suggested that they stop at a nearby island to avoid injury to the other passengers, and the ferry made a detour. As soon as the boat reached the shore, the ruffian leaped off, drew his sword, and assumed his stance. Bokuden stood up and appeared ready to follow his opponent when he suddenly grabbed an oar and precipitately pushed the boat back into the river. He yelled to the stranded ruffian, "This is defeating the enemy without using the sword!"

Unlike many medieval swordsmen who spurned women, Bokuden was happily married with a large family. Near the end of his life, Bokuden had to decide which of his three sons would be his principal heir and become chief instructor of his school of swordsmanship. Bokuden devised the following test: He placed a wooden pillow above the sliding door to his room, balancing it so that it would fall as soon as anyone entered the room, and then summoned each of his sons in turn.

Prior to entering the room, the first son immediately sensed something amiss. He cautiously opened the sliding door, extended his hand, and caught the pillow when it fell. The second son barged right into the room, but managed to dodge the falling pillow. The third son also went straight into the room but he was able to draw his sword and cleave the pillow in two in midair. After observing their behavior, Bokuden made the first son his successor.

A master swordsman had three senior students. He instructed each one to traverse a narrow ravine inhabited by a fierce wild horse. The first student walked right into the ravine and faced the horse head on. He managed to block or evade the flailing hooves and emerged unscathed. The second student, taking notice of the horse's rage, deftly skirted the walls of the ravine, where the horse could not reach him, and also escaped unharmed. When the third student nonchalantly appeared in the ravine, however, the horse immediately calmed down, whinnied an acknowledgment, and paid him no further attention. The third student was made the successor.

Another school of swordsmanship with an unusual name is the Mugan Ryu, the "No Eyes School." The founder of this school, Sorimachi Mukaku (d. 1742), was traveling around the country on a budo quest when he came to a single-log bridge spanning a deep gorge. The log was very narrow, and when Mukoku made a tentative step on it, the log felt slippery. Afraid to attempt the crossing, Mukaku hesitated at the head of the log. Suddenly, a blind traveler appeared, slipped off his sandals, and sauntered across the bridge without the slightest concern. Mukaku realized that he should cross the bridge fearlessly like the blind man, and did so. If one sees with the eyes of the heart rather than the eyes of the head, there is nothing to fear. Later, Mukaku founded the No Eyes School based on this insight.

To increase the speed of their techniques, some martial artists practiced catching sparrows. Using grains of rice as a lure, they would entice the sparrows to come close enough to catch with their hands. Once they were able to catch the birds that way, they hid behind the *shoji* (a sliding paper door) and then attempted to open the door and catch a sparrow in a fell swoop.

There were two master sparrow-catching samurai in old Japan: Teishun and Genban. Genban, however, admitted that Teishun's technique was far superior. Genban almost always killed or injured the birds he grabbed. Teishun, on the other hand, could catch and release a sparrow unharmed; not only that, he could do so without scaring the other birds away.

The Zen master Takuan (1573-1645) was teacher to many famous swordsmen. Iemitsu (1604-1651), the third Tokugawa Shogun, received a tiger as a gift from the Korean court. Iemitsu challenged master swordsman Yagyu Tajima

Munenori (1571–1646) to subdue the beast. Munenori immediately accepted the challenge and strode confidently into the cage. Just as the beast was about to pounce, he thumped the snarling animal on the head with his iron fan. The tiger shrank back and cowered in a corner. Takuan, who was also present, chided Munenori, "That is the wrong approach." Takuan then entered the cage unarmed. When the tiger reared to attack, Takuan spat on his hands and gently rubbed the tiger's face and ears. The ferocious animal calmed down at once, purring and rubbing itself against the monk. "That's how you do it!" Takuan exclaimed.

Iemitsu also had a pet monkey that was extraordinarily agile and clever. Iemitsu wanted to see if any of his swordsmen could hit the monkey, and ordered them to try. The monkey stayed close to the Shogun and none of the swordsmen could strike it with a wooden sword, not even the great Munenori. Takuan was summoned once again, and as soon as he brandished his priest's wooden stick at the monkey, it shrieked and cowered before the Zen master.

"How did you do that?" everyone wanted to know.

"All of the swordsmen held back a bit, in fear that they might hit the Shogun. That didn't concern me at all, and the monkey sensed that there was no way it could escape."

Munenori one day attempted to duplicate the feat of the horseman Magaki Heikuro, who had ridden a horse up and down a steep flight of stone steps. He failed, however, and sought Takuan's advice.

Ho Ge Jaku (read right to left) by Takuan. These three characters mean "Cast everything off!" That was the core of Takuan's teaching to his samurai followers. In order to achieve mastery, one had to cast off attachment both to particular techniques and to notions of self: "Arouse the mind without letting it settle anywhere."

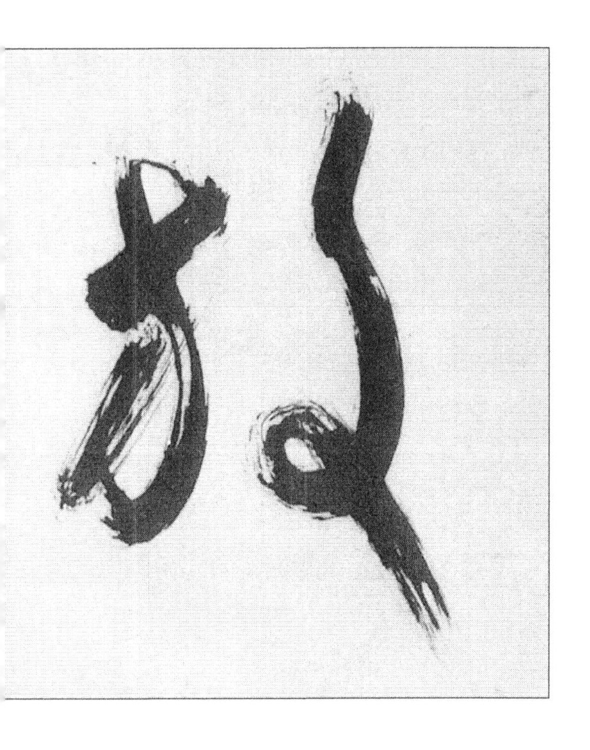

Takuan wanted to give it a try himself and, sure enough, got the horse to gallop up and down the steps. Munenori was nonplussed. "How on earth were you able to do that?"

Takuan answered with a Zen riddle: "No rider on the horse, no horse under the rider."

One day Takuan noticed Iemitsu jumping back and forth from his veranda out into the rain, and asked the Shogun what he was doing.

"I'm perfecting my lightning-fast technique. I'm practicing dodging raindrops. Look, I'm hardly wet."

"Very impressive," Takuan said, "but I am even faster."

"Is that so?" Iemitsu responded. "How about a demonstration?"

Takuan stepped into the garden in his heavy wooden clogs, and got soaking wet.

"What kind of lightning-fast technique is that?" Iemitsu demanded to know.

"When it rains, you get wet. That is natural. Trying to avoid raindrops is a mere stunt, and a foolish waste of time."

Once Takuan was traveling in a remote area of Japan and stopped at an inn to eat. The people there warned Takuan about a group of bandits who were roaming the countryside. Takuan said, "Since they are causing so much trouble I will have to catch them."

"But you are a Zen monk, not a swordsman, so how will you do that?" the people asked.

"There is no danger, they are just human beings. And

besides, if you didn't have so many possessions, there would be nothing for a robber to steal. Think about that." So saying, off Takuan went.

After walking a bit, Takuan reached a small shrine in the woods. Two rough-looking characters were making a fire, and Takuan came up and surprised them with the greeting, "Hey, you two. Are you robbers?"

"Who are you?" they demanded.

"Just a beggar monk."

"What are you doing wandering around here at night?"

"I was about to ask you the same thing. Take me to your chief."

"You mad impudent fool!" the two robbers shouted, reaching for their weapons. Before they could get them out, Takuan struck their hands with his short wooden priest's stick and knocked them down. He quickly tied them up with his priest's belt.

"Don't kill us!" they pleaded.

"Don't worry. I am a monk and I made a vow not to take life. Take me to your chief."

The two bound men took Takuan to their robbers' den. When Takuan strode into the cave, the startled bandit chief cried out, "Who are you?"

"A beggar monk come to capture you," Takuan announced.

The bandit chief grabbed a spear and tried to run Takuan through. Takuan dodged the attack and threw the bandit chief to the ground and pinned him there. Takuan sensed that the man was no common criminal and asked what had happened to cause him to fall so far.

"I used to be a samurai of the Otomo clan. My name is Onoda Kogoro and my father was the famed spear fighter

Onoda Kageya. I was his successor, but I spoke out against the excesses of the leader of the Otomo clan and I was banished. I became a bandit out of desperation. I am so ashamed. I will now commit *seppuku (hara-kiri)* to atone for my violation of the samurai code."

"Wait!" Takuan ordered. "To become a bandit chief, you had to follow the five cardinal virtues of a samurai: You needed wisdom to devise strategy; you needed bravery to accomplish your task; you did your duty as a leader of men; you commanded respect as a fair leader; and you showed benevolence by sharing the bounty. You behaved honorably, after a fashion, so make things right by reforming yourself and becoming a respectable member of society." Kogoro redeemed himself and became a retainer of the Yagyu clan.

Shoju (1642–1721) was another Zen monk well known for "thrashing master swordsmen." One day, a pompous samurai visited Shoju and grandiosely expounded his theories on the art of the sword. Shoju listened politely for a while but then suddenly leaped up and pummeled the samurai unmercifully. "You are full of nothing but hot air!" he exclaimed.

Word of Shoju's startling behavior created a stir, and the Zen master was invited to observe a training session for master swordsmen. The assembled swordsmen doubted that Shoju could defeat any of them without the element of surprise.

They informed Shoju of their doubt, and at once he challenged them to strike. Not one of them was able to hit the Zen master, and all received at least one good rap on the head from his priest's stick. Thoroughly humbled, they asked him his secret.

"If your eye is true, and your mind unobstructed, there is nothing you cannot overcome, including a sword attack."

The temple of the Zen master Hakuin (1686-1768) was located in Hara, along the old Tokai Highway, and a number of provincial lords traveling to and from the capital of Edo stopped by to seek his advice. Once, a lord wanted to know, "What is heaven? What is hell?"

"What's the matter? Are you frightened of hell?" Hakuin sneered. "A sniveling coward like you is not worth teaching. Get out of here right now!"

The lord, who was not accustomed to being insulted and berated by anyone, drew his sword and went after Hakuin. He chased Hakuin into the main hall and struck with blind fury at the Zen master. None of the blows landed, though, and Hakuin disappeared into the shadows.

"This anger is your hell!" Hakuin yelled out from the dark.

The lord calmed down and apologized for losing his temper.

"That apology is heaven," Hakuin said to him.

(Since a samurai had to be perpetually on guard, always properly dressed, and ready to lay down his life at any time, Hakuin once wrote that a devoted samurai could accomplish in one month what it took an untroubled monk a year to do.)

There was at least one Zen priest who was actually a highly skilled martial artist: Takeda Motsugai (1794-1869), founder of the Fusen School of Martial Arts. Nicknamed "The Fist Priest," Motsugai dressed in shabby clothes and was often mistaken for a common beggar. One day, Motsugai passed by a training hall where a group of soldiers were practicing bayonet fighting. Motsugai stopped in to watch and the soldiers took offense, thinking he was mocking them. The drill leader challenged Motsugai to a duel, confident that the ragamuffin monk would be an easy target to practice with a live blade.

"I'm a monk so I cannot use a weapon, but I have these," Motsugai said as he pulled two wooden bowls from his monk's sack.

When the enraged drill leader thrust his bayonet at Motsugai's chest, the monk caught the blade between the two bowls and immobilized the attack. Motsugai then suddenly released his grip and the drill leader went flying back and landed on his rear end. Realizing that the monk was a master martial artist, the drill leader bowed deeply in apology.

It is said that the powerful Motsugai was once held to a draw by a female warrior. Lady Shuei of the Matsudaira clan challenged Motsugai to a duel when she was twenty-seven years old. Her weapon of choice: a one-hundred-fifty-pound iron halberd. Motsugai declared the contest a draw after battling Shuei for a day and a night.

Motsugai was said to be amazingly fleet of foot, a speedy and seemingly tireless walker. He told his disciples, "In order to walk fast you must: walk straight; not be distracted by the view; not walk in a group; lead with the left foot; and swing your hands as you walk."

Once Motsugai was visiting the lord of the Mihara domain, and he was shown a painting of a solitary goose done by an artist in the lord's employ. "Geese always fly in flocks," the displeased lord said to Motsugai, "and I feel that this goose is ignoring his fellow birds." Upon hearing that, Motsugai took out his brush and wrote this inscription on the painting: "This is the head of the flock, more will follow, more will follow." The lord was much happier with the painting.

There were, of course, many Zen masters who were not martial artists. Muso Kokushi (1275-1351) was once traveling with one of his followers, an expert swordsman. As they were boarding a ferry boat, a drunken ruffian rushed up and demanded to be let on the boat even though it was already full to capacity. The ruffian leaped onto the boat and started making waves. Concerned that the boat would capsize, Muso intervened and asked the violent ruffian to sit down. The annoyed ruffian hit Muso on the head with his iron fan. Blood poured down his forehead but Muso did not flinch and got the ruffian to sit down. As soon as they reached the other shore, Muso's traveling companion, the skilled swordsman, stepped from the boat and waited, with his hand on the hilt of his sword, for the ruffian to come ashore. The ruffian realized what was going to happen and shrank back into the boat. Muso intervened once more, pulling his follower away as he said, "Be a good Buddhist. Let him go."

This print by Yoshitoshi (1839-1892) depicts the female budo master Oiko teaching a lesson to the ruffian wrestler Saeki. When Saeki tried to molest the pretty young woman she pinned his arm against her body and dragged him off to her cottage where she made him eat rice balls that she had squeezed into the consistency of rocks. When Oiko finally let Saeki go, however, he discovered that he had gained great strength.

River

This world's
dust and dirt
flows away,
all is purified
by the waves of Kamo River.

Before becoming a Buddhist nun, Otagaki Rengetsu (1791-1875) was trained as a samurai lady. She excelled at both the literary and martial arts.

Purity of heart and a free-flowing spirit are essential elements of budo.

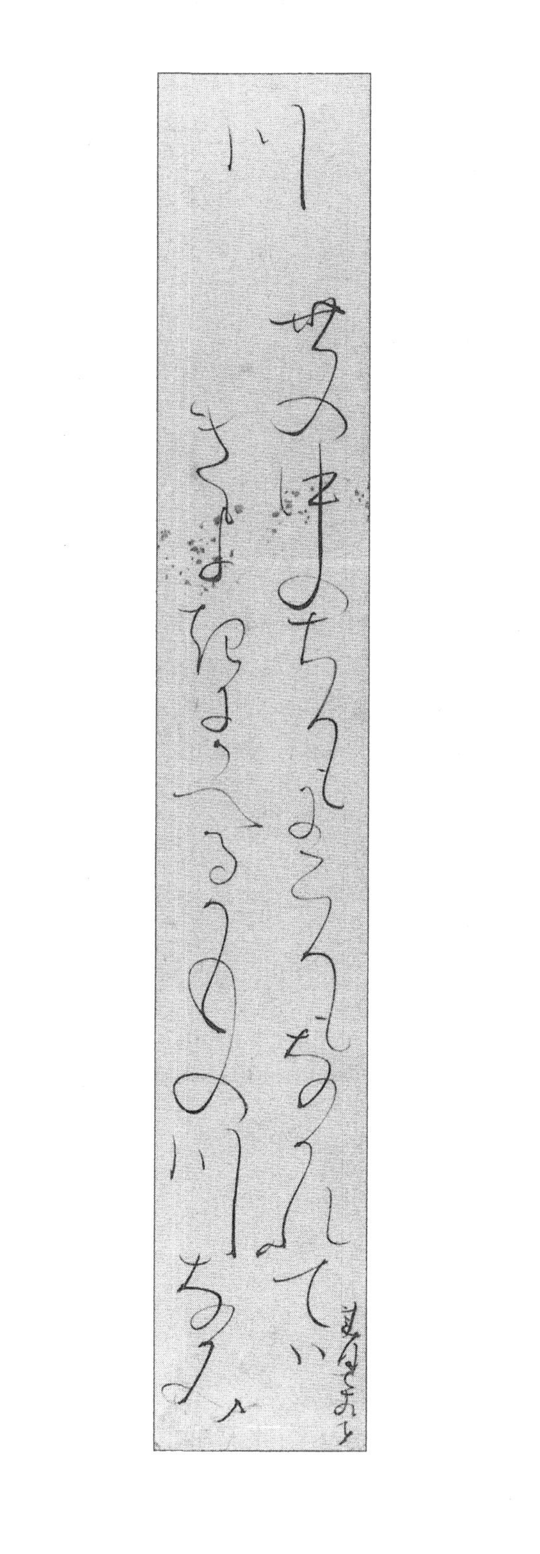

Two lovely and elegantly dressed samurai ladies practice budo in the Shogun's castle. Print by Chikanobu (1838–1912).

Suzuki Seibe'e was a master of the Kito School of Jujutsu. When Lord Sakai heard of Suzuki's reputation as a martial artist, he summoned Suzuki to the castle to see for himself if the rumors were true. The lord selected his strongest samurai and ordered Suzuki to engage him. Informing the lord that "a grappling contest is not a real test," Suzuki asked for a brush and ink to be prepared. He then held a poem card in his left hand and said to his audience:

"I am going to write a poem on this card. I will let my opponent hold my left arm and he is free to apply any technique to it while I write."

Suzuki extended his left arm for his opponent to hold. The opponent seized Suzuki's arm and pushed and pulled, but Suzuki's arm did not seem to budge and he finished the poem. He then showed the card to the lord–the lines of the poem were perfectly straight with no sign of disturbance.

Suzuki let the lord and others hold his left arm while he wrote poems on more cards, but the brushwork was perfect each time. Suzuki smiled and said to them, "This is the essence of *yawara* (the art of flexibility)." Convinced, the lord and his retainers became Suzuki's disciples.

As a master swordsman, Tesshu was often asked to authenticate finely forged blades. Rather than minutely examining the blade and checking the signature of the maker against known examples—a process that can sometimes take months—Tesshu would simply take the sword into the dojo, let out a shout, and swing it two or three times. That would be enough to tell if it was the genuine article or not.

Kyu Zen Ichimi, "The Bow and Zen Are One," calligraphy on a fan, dated "1936, autumn," by Kenzo Awa (1880–1939), the hero of *Zen and the Art of Archery* by Eugen Herrigel. Awa and Herrigel had this Zen dialogue:

"The right art is aimless!" Awa declared.

"How does one learn that?" Herrigel asked.

"By letting go of yourself, leaving yourself and everything yours behind you so decisively that nothing more is left of you but a purposeless tension."

"So I must become purposeless—on purpose?"

"No pupil has ever asked me that, so I don't know the right answer."

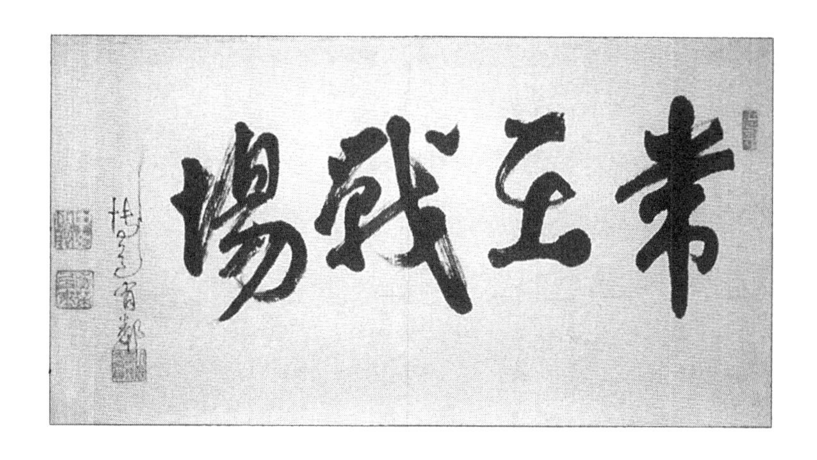

Jozai Senjo, "Always Present on the Battlefield," by Hakudo Nakayama (1895-1958). Hakudo was the father of modern *Iaido*, the art of drawing the sword, and a good friend of Aikido's Morihei Ueshiba and Karate's Gichin Funakoshi. His personal motto was *jozai senjo*—"Always present on the battlefield of life, ready to meet any challenge." Hakudo summed up his philosophy of Iaido in this verse:

Do not cut
Do not be cut
Step out of the way,
And attain
A blissful victory.

Two budo scrolls. Left panel: *Stillness in Movement,* by Jusan. This is one of the keys to mastery of budo: No matter how fast the movement, it must emanate from a calm and quiet core. In nature, stillness in movement is manifested perfectly in a hurricane. Right panel: *Plum Blossoms Open Because of the Frost and Snow,* by Hakudo Nakayama. Lovely plum flowers bloom under the harshest conditions. Adversity does not cause a budo practitioner to wither; it helps him or her flourish.

Tesshu would tell his disciples, "When someone comes to the dojo for a challenge match, take a look at the bottom of his wooden sandals in the entrance hall while he is changing clothes in the hall. If the teeth on the bottom of the sandals are not worn evenly, you can be sure he is often off balance and not much of a swordsman."

Tesshu disliked anyone who attacked another human being's weak point to attain superiority. He said, "In the training hall and in daily life you must never take advantage of another's weakness. Always contest on the highest levels."

In the training hall of Terada Gorozaemon (1744–1825) only prescribed forms *(kata)* were practiced. One day, his senior students asked if they could please engage the master in free-form sparring with bamboo swords. Terada was displeased, since the students obviously felt that kata training was inadequate. Terada allowed them to get suited up in body armor but wore no protection and held a short wooden sword.

The matches began but the instant a student thought, "I'll strike his head," Terada shouted, "Do that and I'll cut through your body!" If the student thought, "No, I'll strike his wrist," Terada countered with, "Try that and I'll cut and thrust." All of the students were thus completely stymied, unable to make a single undetected move.

When asked how he could read their minds, Terada

replied: "The purpose of swordsmanship is to illumine the true nature of life and death. If your mind is bright and pure, free of confusion or malice, it can reflect the thoughts of an opponent as clearly as a mirror." He added, "The secrets of our school are all contained in the kata."

Healing has always been an important aspect of budo, and, on occasion, the healing arts take precedence over the martial arts. Nakura Naoken was a teacher of Yoshin Jujutsu and Shinto Swordsmanship, and he operated a training hall in the Senju District of Edo. Nakura was also highly skilled at *seikotsu-jutsu,* the art of bone-setting (somewhat akin to Western chiropractic treatment). In 1773, there was a huge fire in Edo, and thousands were trampled and injured in the mad rush to escape the flames. Nakura had so many patients to treat that he closed the martial arts training hall and turned it into a full-time clinic. Nakura's system, based on his knowledge of the martial and healing arts, is the source of most of the *seikotsu* technique used today.

Jirokichi Yamada (1863–1931) was a master swordsman of the Jikishin-kage School. It is said that once when Yamada was walking with his teacher Kenkichi Sakakibara (1829–1894), the aging master stumbled on a steep slope. Sakakibara's *geta* (old-style Japanese wooden sandal) flew off but before his foot hit the ground, Yamada had, in an instant, slipped out of his own geta and placed it under Sakakibara's foot. His motto was: "One who is careless in small things is careless in all and will never accomplish great things." Yamada used to stand in the doorway of his training hall, holding a bamboo sword, and observe his students coming to practice. Anyone approaching the hall dragging his feet, or acting in an inattentive manner, got a sharp rap on the shin from Yamada's sword. "Swordsmanship does not begin and end at the gate of the training hall!" Yamada would thunder.

Yamada was a meticulous person. He had all the documents concerning classical swordsmanship that he had received from his teachers wrapped in fire-resistant paper. The documents were stored neatly in a box that could be quickly moved in case of an emergency. He maintained, "It is my duty to preserve these invaluable documents for future generations." When the conflagration caused by the Great Kanto Earthquake in 1923 threatened to engulf Yamada's residence, he immediately removed the box from the shelf and prepared to flee to safety. However, he suddenly thought to himself: "How will it look if people see a samurai running away to protect material possessions? It is foolish to save samurai documents while ignoring the samurai spirit to serve society." Yamada replaced the box and then ran out into the street to help pull people from the rubble and fight the fire. (The documents survived unscathed.)

The swordsman Junichi Haga, a disciple of Hakudo Nakayama, was afraid of no one, and he challenged Morihei Ueshiba, the greatest martial artist of the time (and perhaps all time). Armed with a wooden sword, Haga lashed out at Morihei but the Aikido master disappeared. Haga looked around and found Morihei standing in front of him.

"Convinced?" Morihei asked.

"Not yet!" Haga shouted as he launched a furious attack that continued until he ran out of breath. And he had come nowhere near hitting Morihei.

"Had enough?" Morihei wanted to know.

When Haga shook his head, Morihei held him in an iron grip.

"Can't move, can you?" Morihei said.

"I can still move my feet."

Morihei then pinned Haga to the ground, completely immobilizing his hands and feet.

"Ready to give up now?"

"No, I still can move," insisted Haga.

"What?"

"I still can move my mouth," Haga said.

Morihei smiled and released Haga. "I guess you got the better of me. I like your spirit."

Kanryo Higaonna (1853-1917), considered the father of the Goju-ryu style of Karate, led a frugal life. Even though he had little money, he would not accept payment from his disciples and only allowed them to present him with gifts of food once or twice a year.

Higaonna's disciples felt that such a fine teacher deserved to have a wider student base and suggested that he put out a sign board like all of the other dojo. Kanryo refused: "If I hung a sign board, that would be inviting anyone to come to train and that is unacceptable. Teaching a martial art is like giving someone a weapon. If the wrong person receives that weapon, innocent people can get hurt."

Higaonna's top student was Gojun Miyagi (1888–1953), the actual founder of the Goju-ryu. Miyagi had many students but he would not give any of them *dan* rankings, even though such a ranking system had been adopted by almost every other martial art. Miyagi felt that ranking systems create artificial levels of attainment, and people get judged for their rank, not their character. Miyagi instructed his students to keep the fact that they practiced Karate a secret, in distinct contrast to students of other dojo who boasted of their dan ranks.

Here are some of Miyagi's maxims:

> If your temper rises, withdraw your hand; if your hand rises, withdraw your temper.
>
> The true victory is defeat of your base nature. That triumph is far superior to the conquering of any foe. The ultimate strategy is to win through virtue and perseverance, not by battle.
>
> Heaven, earth, and Karate are one. As the sun rises and sets, as the oceans ebb and flow, so does ki circulate in the human body. Know the relationship between the time of day and the vital points of the body.

The Karate master Kanken Toyama told his students: "Secret techniques begin with basic techniques; basic techniques end as secret techniques. There are no secrets at the beginning, but there are secrets at the end. The key to success is hard training."

In 1947, during the American military occupation of Japan, Toyama was suddenly attacked by a group of drunken American soldiers. During that period, it was futile for Toyama to fight back since he would surely be thrown in prison with a long sentence for injuring an American, even if it were in self-defense. Toyama took all the blows but did not sustain any injuries. In fact, he was barely bruised. Part of traditional Karate training consists of hardening the body and filling it with protective energy for just such an occasion when it is not possible to ward off blows.

Once when Kyuzo Mifune visited a Karate dojo, he was shown a demonstration of "tile-breaking" by one of the Karate men. After the Karate man had smashed a number of tiles piled on top of each other, he asked Mifune, "Can a Judo man do this?"

"Yes, it is very easy," Mifune replied.

"Is that so? Can we see what kind of technique a Judo man uses?" the Karate man challenged.

"Of course. Please set up the tiles. I'll be back in a minute," Mifune instructed.

Mifune returned with a hammer he had brought along in his bag.

"You are not going to use that to break the tiles, are you?" the Karate man protested.

"Yes. I told you it was easy. Efficient use of energy is a key principle of Judo."

Saburo Minaki (1906–1988), seventeenth headmaster of Hontai Yoshin School, was a tiny, frail-looking man. Many martial artists of other schools came to challenge Minaki, not infrequently laughing out loud when they saw him in person. "You are the headmaster?" None could best Minaki, however, and often he scared challengers away by first picking up a rock and smashing it to smithereens with his bare hands. Then he would tell them: "External strength that you can boast of is not real strength; true power is hidden deep inside."

Minaki was very selective about whom he accepted as a disciple: "Budo is a fine art. If you do not want to obtain the mind of a buddha, you will never make a true martial artist."

Rinjiro Shirata was a great teacher of Aikido. When he was a young man, Shirata was sent to Osaka by his teacher Morihei Ueshiba to establish Aikido in that area. One of the key principles of Aikido is *muteiko,* "nonresistance." Shirata was explaining this principle to a group of martial artists when the most powerful member present suddenly leaped up and yelled, "What nonsense! Non-resist this!" The fellow leaped at Shirata but immediately found himself face-down on the mat, pinned like a butterfly. "See what I mean," Shirata said with a smile, "No one can resist nonresistance."

Much later in life, when Shirata was seventy-five years old—he trained right up to the end of his life at age eighty—a professional wrestler named Fujinami appeared at the training hall, accompanied by a sports journalist and a photographer. A professional wrestling show was being held in town that weekend, and the media picked up on rumors of a local old Aikido master. Shirata refused to teach Fujinami at first since he had no formal introduction, but he did allow the professional wrestler, who had come decked out in his trunks, to watch. After a while, Shirata sensed that the wrestler and his party thought the techniques were staged, so Shirata called Fujinami up. Fujinami quickly found himself down, a number of times, and "Grandfather Aikido Master Pins Wrestling Champion" made headlines the next day. Fujinami sent Shirata a polite letter thanking him for his kind instruction.

A longtime acquaintance told me this story about his Kendo teacher.

"My Kendo teacher suffered a stroke and fell into a coma. Since I was on the staff of the hospital I was able to visit him just after he came in. When I arrived in his room, he was making the shouts used in a Kendo contest, even though he was still unconscious. After a bit, he came to, and I asked him with whom he was fighting.

"Emma (the King of Hades)," he told me.

"Who won?"

"I did. I beat the hell out of him," he said with a smile. He died later that evening.

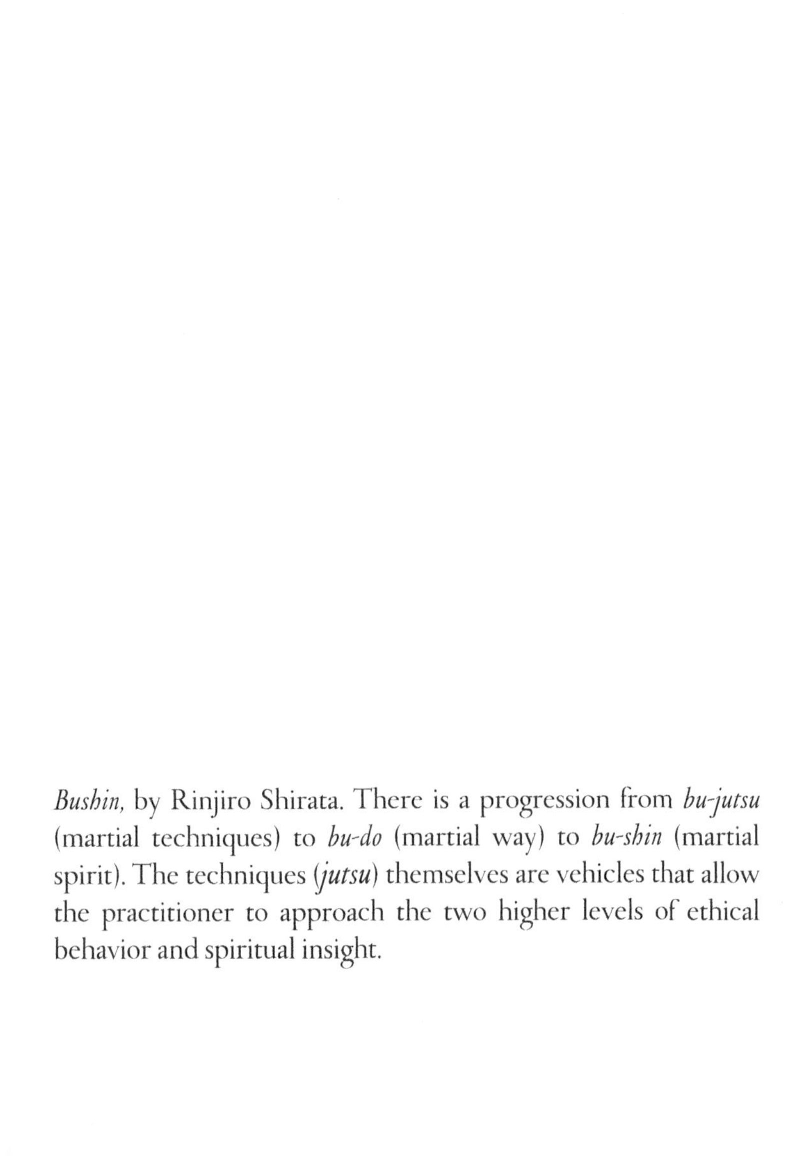

Bushin, by Rinjiro Shirata. There is a progression from *bu-jutsu* (martial techniques) to *bu-do* (martial way) to *bu-shin* (martial spirit). The techniques (*jutsu*) themselves are vehicles that allow the practitioner to approach the two higher levels of ethical behavior and spiritual insight.

武神

SOURCES

IN JAPANESE

Domoto, Akinori, *Nakayama Hakudo Yushinkan.* Tokyo: Shimazu Shobo, 1993.

Imamura, Yoshio. *Nihon kengo shi.* Tokyo: Shinjinbutsu Orai Sha, 1971.

Kaku, Kozo. *Bujutsu budoka retsuden.* Tokyo: Shimazu Shobo, 1999.

Kato, Kanji. *Budo no Kenkyu.* 2 vols. Uchihara: Kato Kanji Zenshu Hanko Kai, n.d.

Kato, Totsudo. *Kenkaku zenwa.* Tokyo: Kokusho Hanko Kai, 1917.

Mifune, Kyuzo. *Judo kaiko roku.* Tokyo: Harubu, 1981.

Misaki, Ryuichiro. *Nakamura Tempu: Gin no kotaba.* Tokyo: KK Bestseller, 1995.

Miyazaki, Mitomo. *Gendai budo zensho.* Tokyo: Shinjinbutsu Orai Sha, 1994.

Nagamine, Shoshin: *Okinawa karate sumo meijin den.* Tokyo: Shinjinbutsu Orai Sha, 1986.

Omori, Sogen. *Ken to Zen.* Tokyo: Shunju Sha, 1973.

Shimada, Akinori. *Gokui to wa nanika: Hiden Neko no Myojutsu.* Tokyo: Bab Japan, 1997.

Takahashi, Michio. *Bushido no rekishi.* 3 vols. Tokyo: Shinjinbutsu Orai Sha, 1999.

Tanaka, Mitsugi. *Bakumatsu Meiji Kenkaku Kengo Sokan.* Tokyo: Shinjinbutsu Orai Sha, 1985.

Terayama, Tanchu. *Gorinsho: Miyamoto Mushashi no waza to michi.* Tokyo: Kodansha, 1984.

Tobe, Shinjuro. *Heiho hidenko.* Tokyo: Shinjinbutsu Orai Sha, 1995.

——. *Kenshi no Meigen.* Tokyo: Kosaido Shuppan, 1998.

Watanabe, Ichiro, ed. *Meji budo shi.* Tokyo: Shinjinbutsu Orai Sha, 1971.

Yoshida, Yutaka. *Budo Hidensho.* Tokyo: Tokuma Shoten, 1968.

IN ENGLISH

Bishop, Mark. *Okinawan Karate.* London: A&C Black, 1989.

Craig, Darrell Max. *The Heart of Kendo.* Boston: Shambhala Publications, 2000.

Deprospera, Dan. *Illumined Spirit: Conversations with a Kyudo Master.* Tokyo: Kodansha International, 1997.

Friday, Karl F., with Seki Humitake. *Legacies of the Sword.* Honolulu: University of Hawaii Press, 1997.

Funakoshi, Gichin. *Karate-do: My Way of Life.* Tokyo: Kodansha International, 1975.

Harrison, E. J. *The Fighting Spirit of Japan: The Esoteric Study of the Martial Arts and Way of Life in Japan.* Woodstock, New York: The Overlook Press, 1988.

Herrigel, Eugen. *Zen and the Art of Archery.* New York: Vintage Books, 1971.

Higaonna, Morio. *The History of Karate: Okinawan Goju-Ryu.* Great Britain: Dragon Books, 1996.

Hirose, Nobuko. *Immovable Wisdom.* Shaftesbury, Dorset, England: Element, 1992.

Kano, Jigoro. *Kodokan Judo.* Tokyo: Kodansha International, 1986.

Krammer, Richard. *Zen and Confucius in the Art of Swordsmanship.* London: Routledge & Kegan Paul, 1978.

Legget, Trevor. *Zen and the Ways*. London: Routledge & Kegan Paul, 1978.

Musashi, Miyamoto. *A Book of Five Rings*. Translated by Victor Harris. New York: The Overlook Press, 1974.

——. *The Book of Five Rings*. Translated by Thomas Cleary. Boston: Shambhala Publications, 1993.

Munenori, Yagyu. *The Sword and the Mind*. Translated by Hiroaki Sato. Woodstock, New York: The Overlook Press, 1986.

Soho, Takuan. *The Unfettered Mind: Writings of the Zen Master to the Sword Master*. Translated by William Scott Wilson. Tokyo: Kodansha International, 1986.

Stevens, John. *The Essence of Aikido: Spiritual Teachings of Morihei Ueshiba*. Tokyo: Kodansha International, 1993.

——. *The Philosophy of Aikido*. Tokyo: Kodansha International, 2001.

——. *The Sword of No-Sword: Life of the Master Warrior Tesshu*. Boston: Shambhala Publications, 1994.

——. *Three Budo Masters: Kano, Funakoshi, Ueshiba*. Tokyo: Kodansha International, 1995.

——. *Zen Masters: Ikkyu, Hakuin, Ryokan*. Tokyo: Kodansha International, 1999.

Sugawara, Makoto. *Lives of Master Swordsmen*. Afterword by John Stevens. Tokyo: The East Publications, 1999.

Suzuki, Daisetsu. *Zen and the Japanese Culture*. Princeton, New Jersey: Princeton University Press, 1970.

Tzu, Chuang. *The Texts of Taoism*. 2 vols. Translated by James Legge. New York: Dover Publications, 1962.